Crossing the Bridge to Hope and Heaven

Patricia Ann Hill

TRILOGY CHRISTIAN PUBLISHERS

Tustin, CA

Trilogy Christian Publishers
A Wholly Owned Subsidary of Trinity Broadcasting Network
2442 Michelle Drive
Tustin, CA 92780

Crossing the Bridge to Hope and Heaven

Rights Department, 2442 Michelle Drive, Tustin, CA 92780.

Trilogy Christian Publishing/TBN and colophon are trademarks of Trinity Broadcasting Network.

For information about special discounts for bulk purchases, please contact Trilogy Christian Publishing.

Trilogy Disclaimer: The views and content expressed in this book are those of the author and may not necessarily reflect the views and doctrine of Trilogy Christian Publishing or the Trinity Broadcasting Network.

Manufactured in the United States of America

10 9 8 7 6 5 4 3 2 1

Library of Congress Cataloging-in-Publication Data is available.

ISBN: 978-1-68556-040-9

E-ISBN: 978-1-68556-041-6

Dedication

This book is dedicated to my son.

While I know my son will never read these words of love, they overflow from my heart and must be released.

My son, you were a gift from heaven upon your birth, a joy brought into existence. You were loved and adored by all who had a hand in your upbringing. There was only one you.

As an early teen, you accepted Christ as Savior and used your spiritual gift for the body of Christ because you loved to assist people. Later in life you felt it necessary to rededicate your life to Jesus Christ and was re-baptized. You chose not to share that moment with us because you said it was between you and the Savior. You confessed and surrendered. There was no going back and no detours ever again.

You faced many roadblocks and challenges all of which you pushed through and overcame. There was only one you. You never let your faith in God waver, and He never left you alone. You prayed, we prayed, and God answered. Our world would stop rotating just to make sure you were okay, whatever it took, because of our love for you. There was only one you.

Your storytelling brought interest and boredom to all. A story or event that began with interest could last minutes or last hours before the ending or punchline. We all endured it because there was only one you. You were warm-hearted and considered everyone as family. "Hey, family," was extended to all whether or not they were actually your family.

Then there is your immediate family. Nothing of life's journey could separate this familial bond. No mountain too high or valley too low. The love was deep and real. You lived with their existence and well-being in mind. A love in your heart that was taken with you to heaven. There was only one you.

Illness then entered the picture and caused your body to fail. Your prayer life was right on point, your Bible was on the bed stand, and while you could not get to church, TBN was the alternative. You fought to live until the Lord said, "It is time to come home my child."

In the presence of your family village you slipped from this earthly life to eternal life in Christ.

This book is dedicated to you, my son, in love and affection.

I would be remiss if I did not also dedicate this book to all who have lost someone so precious in their lives. I hope that you will read this book and interject your own story and journey through your grief process. I pray that you will find peace and wholeness in your spirit and look toward the future with a purpose, a testimony, and a witness to share.

Lovingly, A Mother

Many Thanks

To my sister-in-law, an Evangelist, who walked this walk with me in love, faith, and the Word of God. She grieved along with me and sat while I cried.

To the Preacher of the Gospel, my friend, and sister in Christ, who ministered to me daily through the long days and dark nights of my immense sorrow. Her counsel was invaluable.

I am eternally grateful to both of you.

Thank you to the family who always provided support for my son. He loved you dearly. Sometimes it takes a village. The village was you.

I also extend my love and gratitude to everyone that prayed and encouraged my heart during this journey.

Contents

Preface

Let me introduce myself. I am a mother who birthed one child. There came a day that my child, my son, died at 48 years old. A day that I will seemingly never forget. Unexpected, yes. In the midst of my intense grief, I searched for a book that someone wrote through which I could identify. Let me be clear: I am a Christian. God is my Father. Jesus is my Savior and the Holy Spirit is my helper. The Lord is first in my life.

Being perfectly honest, after my son's death reading the Word of God was a struggle. My Hallelujah was broken, and my prayers were forced. I wandered in the wilderness. When you read my story, you will understand. I did search for a book written by someone who understood what I was experiencing. I thought that reading their story would help me through the days ahead. I found none. It took quite some time for me to get from point A to point B. It was not a sprint but a journey.

When you lose a loved one, people with good intentions will say what they think is appropriate to comfort you. Some words bring comfort, others just irritate.

One such phrase was presented over and over: "God left you here for a purpose, a reason." Be aware that I experienced family death in the past. Over the years my family one by one left this life on earth on a flight to eternal life with Jesus Christ, my mother, father, siblings, husband, then my son. When I visit the cemetery and leave through the exit gate, I feel a sense of dread and sadness still today. Their earthly bodies are there, their souls are with the Lord, and I am heading home.

It took over a year before I came to realize that God did have a purpose, a ministry, a word for me to share. I could not understand, conceive, or predict that one day the Lord would reveal the first glimpse as He raised me out of the ashes. Then it became clear; I had to share my story and encourage another in their deep, gut-wrenching grief.

A friend suggested I write what I was experiencing as each day passed after the loss, and I am passing that wisdom on to you. Write what you are feeling as you grieve, the events, the beginning of healing. While I could not share this with you earlier, I can now. Isaiah 61:3 (KJV), "To appoint unto them that mourn in Zion, to give unto them beauty for ashes, the oil of joy for mourning, the garment of praise for the spirit of heaviness, that they might be called trees of righteousness, the planting of the LORD that he might be glorified."

Please accept my deepest sympathy for your loss. God has not forsaken you. He has not left your side. The angels that He has appointed unto you are in your presence. God has collected each tear you have shed or are still shedding. The Word tells us that God keeps "track of all my sorrows. You have collected all my tears in your bottle. You have recorded each one in your book" (Psalm 56:8, NLT).

I invite you to read my story and put your story in perspective. At the end of each chapter in this book, I implore you to write and reflect on your journey through grief. Know the Lord, Jesus Christ, is with you always and that you are not alone as you are crossing the bridge to hope and heaven.

Journey Through Grief: My Story

As you read this account, know it is raw emotion. I wrote this starting the morning after my son's death and continued to write day after day—most in present tense.

Who would have thought that I would experience extreme, unprepared, excruciating grief again in a lifetime? The loss of my only birth son. Yes, there could have been other times in his life that he would have been snatched from life to life, cancer, and the aftermath, sarcoid, glaucoma, Guillain Barre Syndrome, or the results of an earlier lifestyle since past. But who would know that on October 31, 2019, at the age of 48, a blood clot would begin wreaking havoc within his body? And yes, I was the last of the family to find out about it, the last to arrive at the hospital. His mom was not present from the onset.

[narrative break to being at the hospital]

Twenty-eight plus hours later, he would be with the Lord. This I am sure of because he was sure of it. He had assurance that when he left this earthly presence he would spend eternity with Jesus, and yes, I am assured also. It still does not make this process any easier.

I am not okay. I hurt. I am fumbling with the thought and reality that he is gone from this life. Never to talk to him nor see him again. I know I need to have a heavenly perspective since life on this side is temporary, however, I am still in the flesh, and it is not easy. I cry repeatedly, and no one can ease my pain, my grief. I know in my head that God can, but He has not shown Himself yet to the extent that I need Him. I could not pray or praise Him. Mandissa has a song, "Broken Hallelujah," and that is where I have been. My praise is shattered, my freedom of worship stunted. God, where is your comfort?

[narrative break to present day]

I had a daydream of a supernatural event occurring before his death. I rebuked the thought from my mind by the blood of Jesus, yet it happened. The dream that threw me off the back of someone and waking up on the floor in a fetal position, hurting physically, later bruises to prove it. There was no fear or evil in it. I do not understand how a dream while asleep could manifest itself in the physical. God has not revealed it, and maybe He never will. Just a sign of upcoming dread and destruction of life? I did tell my son about it. He was as baffled as I was. He nor I saw his impending death, just the dream and the lingering after affects.

[narrative break at hospital]

I came into that waiting room where the family was anxiously awaiting news about their most precious loved one. At that time everyone only knows that his heart had stopped more than once. The doctors are working on him. What did that mean at the time? "Working on him"? I believed that God would answer prayers, my child will not die. He will live by the authority in Jesus' name given us. We pray. His pastor came to pray with us as well. Finally, we are able to see him two by two, although most of us went in. When I saw his room number was 'three' (3) I immediately thought of the Godhead's presence; three in one; God the Father, God the Son, God the Holy Spirit. *He will be alright.*

My son's heart stops for the seventh time. In my sanctified mind I think the number seven is perfect because it represents the number of completion. *My child will be healed.* What a terrible sight. The entire family goes into Room #3. The doctors and nurses cannot stop us. This is our son, father, love of his life and brother. While the doctors are giving him manual CPR, some of us pray, some in the Spirit, others speaking to him to fight. *Come on. Fight.* We know he hears, and he fights back to us one more time.

The doctor suggests that we should let him go next time. My answer is an unequivocal 'no.' As long as my son fights for life, the medical staff is to do the same. They agree because a mother's fierceness is not to be reckoned with at such a time as this. The medical team has to get him stable enough to move to ICU. A CAT Scan is the next course of action but could not be done. His condition is too unstable. He is given blood thinners, but the thought is that the blood clot already dissipated.

The family is in the emergency room and then moved to the hallway crying. Some on their knees praying and trying to make sense of this moment. *What is going on? Is God going to answer our prayers? Where are you, God?* I stand watching the family's reactions. One family member on his knees crying and praying, another in the corner clutching his chest, yet another hugging and crying with others. All are praying though. *What is going on God?*

I keep calling my sister-in-law and a close pastor friend, who are both my prayer partners. I want my son to live, to recover. Is that selfish? I am having earthly thoughts with no heavenly meaning or understanding. Then the heart wrenching thought creeps in, *What was my child experiencing in his conscious moments? Was he talking to God? God, where are you? What is all the commotion I am hearing? Familiar voices of family encouraging me? Praying for me? Is that what I am hearing? My body hurts. My chest is in excruciating pain. Or did God spare him from the feeling of pain at that time?* We will never know.

[narrative break]

As I am writing this, grief hurts. In the book *The Shack* the father experiences the great sadness in his grief. That is a good analogy of what I was experiencing right then. It was so great of a sadness that I could hardly bear it. I searched the internet for words of help, nothing to be found. Even the Bible, the story of Job, the widow of Nain, the mother whose son was raised by the prophet, Jairus daughter, Lazarus. Where is my story? No one stepped in. *God, why not heal him?*

My son prayed for healing from Guillain-Barre Syndrome. I knew in my heart of the answer from God. I was just not there yet to accept it or deal with it. I could not stop crying, could not sleep, did not want to go to work or even church. Others have lost children, but their story is not my story. I know they experienced grief maybe even more heart wrenching than mine because of how death occurred. I knew I should have looked at this experience differently, as a child of the Most-High God. I will get there, just not yet.

[narrative break]

The medical staff reveal that my son's heart stopped two more times while getting him settled in the ICU. It is quite some time before we can see him again. There is anticipation and fear each time an update comes from the doctor. Then it comes time to see him. He has a breathing respirator down his throat, and a thousand tubes and bags of medicine are attached to him. The kidney doctor tells us they are going to start dialysis; his organs are failing. The hope is that this will help. A needle is placed in his neck for the dialysis. The blood drips. Other family members come in, and the chaplain is near our side. Conversations had in the waiting room try to remain normal. Everyone is taking turns to see my child, and all are leaving the room heartbroken. About 12:00–1:00 a.m. everyone starts to go home and plan to come back in the morning.

Is God going to heal him? Will he recover? The Bible is full of stories of healing. Can God do it? Most definitely, yes. But will He do it? I am not as sure as I was when I first arrived at the hospital. My son makes it through to another day. God answered.

My son's immediate family—his daughter, her mom, and me—stay the night. We had encouraged his son to drive back to college to take a test as he was graduating in December. I check on my son. His body is breathing hard by the mechanics of the machine, blood on his neck dripping from the dialysis needle. Tubes and more intravenous hook ups have been attached. There are four nurses by his side continually aiding him and the doctor assigned to him is always close by the door. I am helpless. Looking into the room my child looks like he is convulsing, seizing, with his body jerking. *Oh, my God. That is my child. God, where are you? What is going on?* I run back to the waiting room and get on my knees by the chair and try to pray. *What is happening? What is going on? God, Help!*

Then there is a shift in the atmosphere. No longer can I say, "He will live and not die." No longer can I be assured that by the stripes of Christ my child will be healed. Something is changing. I have no confidence that God is going to say 'yes' to my request for Him to save my son. The 'no' is becoming more prevalent in my spirit. Then the shift starts to materialize. *God, I now am turning this over to You. I have to succumb to Your will. I can-*

not tell the family or say out loud my child will live and not die.
Oh my, how this is not a good thing.

I sit for a while then go back into his room. I ask the
nurses to step aside so I can speak into my son's ears.
I tell him I am there, I love him, the family has been
here, and we love him. Then he rustles a little and his
eyes start to blink. He opens his eyes slightly and tries
to turn his head toward me. My child hears me, at least
to some level of understanding. His right hand is moving and trying to communicate. I cannot understand
so I run to the waiting room, and I wake up the love of
his life for the last 24 years. If anyone could understand
him, it would be her. She understands what he is trying
to communicate. He is trying to point to the tubes on
his left side. She asks if he is in pain. He communicates
with his head and eyes, "Yes."

In this moment we learn that the doctor has sedat-
ed him but not with heavy pain medicines. They have
not been sure of his brain activity all this time since
his heart has stopped so many times. The doctor asks
my son some simple commands and he responds. It
is confirmed that his brain is working. They cover his
hands with gauge gloves to protect him from his own
movements.

He wakes up slightly again while we are there and
points toward his heart. We understand him this time.

He is in pain. The doctor finally gives him a Fentanyl drip to ease his pain. It runs through my mind, *Does that mean he has been in pain all these hours or was God merciful and masked the pain?* I will never know.

[narrative break]

Today, December 13, 2019, is the day before my grandson graduates from college. His dad was so proud of him. How I wish he could be here to witness this extraordinary event. God has plans for both of his children, plans that their father will not witness.

At this point in time, I have not cried for two days. Progress? I realized while talking to family members yesterday that life goes on, people move on, and I am still in the same place mourning my son.

[narrative break]

[Now, back to the hospital.]

The doctors give my son an increased dose of pain meds. His body is not rebounding. In the morning we wait to talk to the team of doctors; they try to be sympathetic, to say the right words. But I get where they are going. Apparently, there is acid buildup still happening, medications are being tried, but the medicine is not working. The flesh of my flesh is slipping away.

The family is back in the waiting room and new ones have joined. Eventually, decisions have to be made. By this point I know that I can only ask God to be merciful to my child. I wonder what he is thinking and if there is still a level of consciousness. *Is he making his peace with God knowing he is dying?* My child is going through something that should have been put on me. I am his mom. I should have been able to take the brunt of the pain of his failing body.

The doctors explain the numbers on the screen behind the desk in the hallway. A number associated with the blood pressure that should not go below 59. We wait for a miracle. A miracle that will not happen. He will not be restored to good health at least on earth. I hurt. My child is slipping away. A killer lurked within his body. I am not ready to let him go, and neither is anyone else. This, though, is my story.

[narrative break]

Moving ahead to Saturday morning, December 21st, while lying in bed thinking about a puzzle. When my husband passed it was summer, my favorite time of the year. The back patio beautiful with flowers, some bought by him, which was a yearly ritual. Puzzles, piece by piece, allowed me to focus on something else. It helped me get through the summer. Now after my son's death, pieces do not match up easy. I am not talking about the puzzle but the journey of life. What are the pieces? Where do I start? What is the final picture? What is the purpose going forward?

After my son passed, people would say, "God has a purpose and plan for your life." At my age, what could possibly be the purpose now? The slate is blank. What is the picture on the first piece of the puzzle? Does it start in the middle of the ultimate picture? If so, then consider these words: shock, disbelief, hurt, sadness, no, great sadness, tears, emptiness, heartache, void. Where are the words that are meaningful from the Bible? When in the state of intense grief do the words really resonate in my soul? God seems distant, although I know He is near. Nearer than I want to admit.

I do see the effects of his passing; family members making life changing decisions such as joining church fellowship; a commitment to a new members class, becoming part of the music ministry, participating in a play, decisions to usher. Oh, how he would have loved to have seen this while he was still on this side of heaven. He would be pleased, even now.

I cry less now but still hurt and am sad. I know it will get better. Losing a loved one hurts, but a son? I think about the loss then cry all over again. My chest hurts. Is it my heart, literally?

Christmas is around the corner, four days away. First one in 48 years without my child. I have to get myself together because I need to celebrate the birth of the Child Jesus. God's son. I am often reminded as I grieve that God's son died a horrible, painful death on the cross for my son and for his salvation.

The Bible is sitting to my left on the table. Why am I not reading and studying it? I used to before the passing. What do I read that will comfort me? Maybe start with the Psalms. David grieved. What did he pen?

God, what happened? Why now? I guess the answer would be why not now. We think it was too soon for a child's death, from a parent's perspective. Maybe God was gracious to us and extended his life. He had cancer as an adult. He could have died then but that was not the chosen time. A few months before the passing, my son was diagnosed with Guillain Barre Syndrome. I am starting to believe that God allowed this rare syndrome to manifest so that their relationship would be in a good place when leaving this earthly life.

Puzzle pieces. More puzzle pieces.

My sister-in-law reminded me how I was focused over the last year or so with him going to church consistently to hear the Word of God. How I kept asking him about the relationship he had with the Lord. The only way he would know Him is to study the Word, hear the preached word. Was the fervency of my pushing and pointing out, reminding, and Sunday morning texts "Church?", was it the Holy Spirit preparing him for the transition? Will God reveal or illuminate so I will know?

Nevertheless. A word Jesus used in the garden of Gethsemane. He was on his way to calvary. He knew His purpose on earth in the body given Him by the Father was nearing the end. Jesus went to pray. When He went a little farther, He prayed "O my Father, if it be possible, let this cup pass from me, nevertheless not as I will, but as thou wilt" (Matthew 26:39, KJV). Although I did not use 'nevertheless' when I prayed in the waiting room in the mid of night, I knew I had to leave my child to God's will. I felt the shift in the circumstances; he will live and not die to the nevertheless moment, this was out of my hands. The prayers for his life on earth were becoming futile. This is the second time that I am aware in my life when God's answer was "No." The first was the Christian bookstore I owned that had to close, but that is a story for another day. I knew God was going to heal him. *This is my son Lord. I prayed based on the Bible; You said if I ask anything in the name of Jesus, You will do it.* I could speak to this mountain be thou removed and be cast into the sea, believing and He would give it. Where was the miracle?

I know the age of miracles is not over. The family needs to see the hand of God, Jesus' touch upon my son's body to heal him. During those moments I forgot that "for to me to live is Christ, and to die is gain" (Philippians 1:21, KJV). I forgot that my child prayed while in pain from Guillain-Barre Syndrome for the Lord's healing of his body. Was death the answer to his prayer? The end of suffering and pain on this side of heaven? Seems I have more questions than answers. Lord give me peace in my soul and the answers to the questions. Will the shattered pieces of my heart be made whole? The Word does say in Psalm 23:3, (KJV), "He restoreth my soul."

As death crept closer, we sang "Blessed assurance," which is a hymn my son loved and knew. We quoted the 23rd Psalm. Did he hear them and receive a sense of peace? I wonder why God did not give us the opportunity to converse with him during this time. Sometimes you get the opportunity to say goodbye, to say, "I love you," and have the person return the same. I did not get that privilege with my mom, dad, one of my brothers, nor my husband.

In church one Sunday in January, God brought to my remembrance that my son surrendered. It was like an audible voice. That was a gift from the Lord just for me.

Here I was praying during the ordeal that God would heal my son in front of the family so they would see the power of the Lord through God's healing. But, through this unexpected death, they could see their current state. Are they saved? If that were them close to death, would they be ready when death knocked on their soul? Where would they spend eternity? My son was prepared. Are they? Are we?

The fog of grief is starting to lift. These past two months were my walk through the wilderness, the shadow of death. Whereas I could not pray, praise, worship, or read the Word. This is finally changing. I need the Holy Spirit's help to move from the valley of the shadow of death.

Fast forward to October 28th, days before the first anniversary of my son's death. The closer it comes, the more I mourn and hurt. As the clock moves to this new day, I have an intense moment of remorse, needing forgiveness for the times being a great mom was not part of who I was. Regret sets in. Could I have done better? I ask God if he is okay. I cry and cry, sitting on the steps overlooking the living room. I cry and feel I need forgiveness. I can receive it from God, but I never asked my son, "How can I be a better mom?" Now it is too late. Remembering the last time I saw him, on a walker as he recovered from Guillain Barre Syndrome, coming up the outside steps to my house. We spent quality time together not knowing it is to be the last time. My last text discussion with my only child was on this date a year ago.

[text message]

His text said, "Just was calling to say Goodnight, Love...." My response was, "Going to bed. Have a blessed and restful night, Love mom 🌷"

That was our last communication per my remembrance.

Today is the first anniversary of passing from life to eternal life. All month I have been living in anticipation of this day. Weeping, crying, mentally returning to the hospital, reliving the events of a year ago.

Now, today is the anniversary. I am hurting. This year went quickly. I am grateful for the outreach from friends and family as the date got closer. People remembered and reached out. I spent that day with family celebrating the life of the only son I birthed. Goodbye, my child. I will see you in the morning.

Journal Pages

_____

_____

_____

_____

_____

_____

_____

_____

_____

_____

_____

_____

_____

_____

_____

_____

_____

_____

_____

_____

_____

_____

_____

_____

_____

_____

_____

_____

_____

_____

_____

_____

_____

_____

_____

_____

_____

_____

_____

_____

_____

_____

_____

_____

_____

_____

_____

_____

_____

_____

_____
_____
_____
_____
_____
_____
_____
_____
_____
_____
_____
_____
_____
_____
_____
_____
_____
_____

_____

_____

_____

_____

_____

_____

_____

_____

_____

_____

_____

_____

_____

_____

_____

_____

_____

_____

_____

_____

_____

_____

_____

_____

_____

_____

_____

_____

_____

_____

_____

_____

_____

_____

_____

_____

_____

_____

_____

_____

_____

_____

_____

_____

_____

_____

_____

_____

_____

_____

_____

_____

_____

Crossing the Bridge

Life has invited us on an ever-changing voyage. It is a personal one. We do have traveling companions but then at a point in time we turn around and realize we are now traveling alone. This is our experience; most cannot identify with what we are going through or have been through. So, we put one foot in front of the other and slowly start to walk. Does this sound familiar?

I recall the "Widow of Nain" in Luke 7:11-12 (KJV), "And it came to pass the day after, that he went into a city called Nain; and many of his disciples went with him and much people. Now when he came nigh to the gate of the city, behold, there was a dead man carried out, the only son of his mother, and she was a widow: and much people of the city was with her."

In these verses we meet a mother, merely introduced to us as "the widow of Nain." There is no long dissertation of introduction, no lengthy description of her character, or if she was even a woman of God. We do not know much about her, but what we do know is that she was a mother who lost her only son. That in itself tells us volumes. She is walking alongside or behind her only son's body as it is being carried. She is putting one foot in front of the other and moving forward because she must do so. I am not done referencing this mother and the compassion that Jesus had for her. She will appear again in a later chapter in this book because her story does not end with verse 12.

The Holy Spirit gave me the title for this book. Crossing a bridge is an appropriate description of linking the initial impact of losing someone so precious in our lives to a level of acceptance and resolve. Please know, my fellow traveler, that we can find divine peace and comfort, as we mourn, through our faith in Jesus Christ. "The Lord is close to the brokenhearted and saves those who are crushed in spirit" (Psalm 34:18, NIV).

A bridge is a structure that is built over a body of water, a path, a low place, or another obstacle. It is constructed for the purpose of providing passage over something, usually something that is otherwise difficult or impossible to cross. It allows us to cross from one side to the other. There is a starting point and a destination at the end of it.

Jesus, the bridge in life, supports us over deep waters, the low places, the valleys. When we are at our lowest, the low place of discouragement, anxiety, depression, sorrow, regrets, or the feeling of sinking; this state of mind and emotion swings open a door for the Lord to walk in and show up.

In moments of grief, we can sink to a low place. You have been there at some point in time, haven't you? Even in the valley, we can be assured that God does not plan for us to stay there. There is a Bridge that will carry us to the other side. Deuteronomy 31:8 (NIV), "The LORD himself goes before you and will be with you; he will never leave you nor forsake you. Do not be afraid; do not be discouraged."

There are testimonies in Scripture that we can reference to know for sure that God can do wonders when we are in a low place.

David, a man after God's own heart, experienced being discouraged, depressed and sorrowful. He lost a son. Read 2 Samuel 18:33 (KJV), where his grief is expressed: "And the King was much moved, and went up to the chamber over the gate, and wept." David testifies in Psalm 116:6 (NIV), "The LORD protects the unwary; when I was brought low, he saved me."

Another testimony is the book of Ruth. In the first chapter of the book of Ruth we meet a woman named Naomi. The Bible says there was a famine in the land. Naomi and her two sons, led by her husband, left Bethlehem in Judah to live in the land of Moab for a while. After being settled there, her husband dies. Living in Moab about 10 years, her sons die. Here is a woman, who for 'a while,' was escaping a dismal situation with her family to embrace a more promising existence. There was food in Moab. Can you imagine her pain and anguish? Yes, I guess you can. Naomi, in her pain and loss, stood at the entrance of a corridor and decided to start her journey to Bethlehem. Unbeknownst to her at the time, this corridor would lead to a future of hope.

"For I know the thoughts that I think toward you, says the LORD, thoughts of peace, and not of evil, to give you a future and a hope" (Jeremiah 29:11, NKJV).

There are essential parts of a bridge structure. First and foremost, there is the foundation. The foundation connects the structure to the ground and transfers the load of it to the ground below. I draw an analogy between the elements of constructing a suspension bridge and our journey across the bridge to hope and heaven.

A bridge carries an enormous amount of weight. Suspension bridges use several construction elements to ensure a safe passage for travelers. A road is laid across cables which are threaded together with the correct balance of forces, so it will not buckle or snap under pressure. It is strengthened by framework that runs underneath the road allowing heavier weights and loads to be transported across.

A solid foundation is crucial to support a bridge. Once secure, layer upon layer can be constructed. In Luke 6:47-48 (NLT), Jesus describes a wise builder, one of which we are to identify and emulate.

> I will show you what it's like when someone comes to me, listens to my teaching, and then follows it. It is like a person building a house who digs deep and lays the foundation on solid rock. When the floodwaters rise and break against that house, it stands firm because it is well built.

A builder who is wise, hears the Word of God and can apply it to their life during unsettled times. Our spiritual foundation is vital, especially when we are struggling to stay afloat. Trusting God, along with our personal relationship with Christ and the power of the Holy Spirit plus applying God's Word are all key to building a solid foundation of faith. I have a picture on my wall that says, "Spirit lead me where my Trust is without borders." When tempests of life come our way, when the wind is knocked out of us, biblical truths still stand tall. I can testify that it was hard and seemingly impossible to be steady as a rock and grounded when the floodwaters of loss beat me down. But deep down in my soul I knew I could rely on God's strength and trust His sovereignty. God is in control whether I doubted it or not at times. He is in control. I was weak with little strength to meet the dawn of the next day. Then I remembered I am His and His "power is made perfect in weakness" (2 Corinthians 12:9, NIV). In my weakness.

There is a hymn brought to mind written by Edward Mote a pastor in England in 1834, the latter verses:

> *His oath, his covenant, his blood*
> *Supports me in the whelming flood*
> *When all around my soul gives way,*
> *He then is all my hope and stay*
> *On Christ the solid rock I stand*
> *All other ground is sinking sand*
> *All other ground is sinking sand.*

Suspension bridges were named as such because the road is suspended by cables connected to two towers, on either end to take the strain and weight. Those cables transfer the tension and compression unto the tower. The pure length of a suspension bridge means many forces are at work to secure it and to transfer the weight to a stronger area that can handle the pressure.

I refer you to Proverbs 18:10 (KJV), "The name of the Lord is a strong tower: the righteous runneth into it, and is safe."

Calling on the name of the Lord, I find a merciful God. He loves me, He loves you, even if we distance ourselves and cry out multiple times: *Why? Where were you, Lord? Help!* Grief can take us places where we never thought we would go. Yet, there is still a place the Lord offers us to rest in Him. He may never reveal the mystery of the 'why,' but know for sure He never stepped away; in my case, I did.

When I visualize God as my strong tower, I see in Him a place where I am safe, set above and hidden from the pain and sorrow that overwhelms me. Even if I only allow myself to stay there for a moment. He is my refuge, our refuge. A place of comfort. When our faith is only the size of a grain of mustard seed (Matthew 17:20), with that grain we can speak to the mountain of grief that seems insurmountable. I will get through this, if only with my grain of faith, leaning on the strong tower with the assurance that healing and hope is waiting for me.

Drawing again upon an analogy of the elements of a suspension bridge and our journey across the bridge to hope and heaven, most bridges have mile markers. This allows the traveler to identify the distance from the beginning to a destination. These markers are intentionally spaced at the same distance apart from each other. They are meant to provide some comfort for those stranded because these markers allow emergency responders to locate anyone in need of their help or assistance. I can say without doubt that Jesus Christ is our emergency responder.

My "Mile Markers" are the chapter titles in this book. The processing of my son's passing will not be the same as yours in the loss of your loved one. The distance between each marker was longer for me in the beginning. I had to face the immediacy of my son's death, reliving over and over each detail of all he went through during the preceding hours. Reliving the nine times he coded, my shock, my despair, and my heartbreak.

Crossing the bridge has to start somewhere in order to reach the destination of healing and acceptance. As I said earlier, the process is not a sprint, it is a journey. What are your "Mile Markers," and how are you making it through this most difficult time? Or are you just starting? I encourage you to write your story in the journal pages. It may help you to put pen to paper to reveal how you are processing the loss, the emptiness, the low places, denial, the regrets and ever flowing tears. It may help for you to reach the next "Mile Marker." Write how with each step you take; you pick up the pace as you begin to realize you are not walking alone. The Lord is by your side, sometimes even carrying you. There is a poem about footprints in the sand. At first, two set of footprints are seen as the journey begins, then there was only one set of footprints that appeared when the sorrow was heavy. The traveler asked the Lord about it. "I needed you. Where did you go?" And the Lord responded, "When you only saw the one set of footprints, it was because I carried you."

There does come a point in time when you can see the light before you. The sunrise warms your spirit. You feel alive again. Writing my story has truly helped me rise out of the ashes. I am on my way to becoming whole again.

You will be whole again, as well.

Mile Marker #1: The Shadow of Death

Some people equate their journey through loss and grief as a wilderness wandering or a desert experience. That is certainly a true comparison.

As the great sadness was fresh in my sight, my mind and spirit placed me in a desert-like atmosphere. It was like crawling on hands and knees through a sandstorm. This was a place where I could not see my way clear. Tear droplets mixed with particles of sand blocking vision. *In what direction am I heading?* Seemingly pushing against the wind of grief. Some moments giving up and laying prostrate, other times crawling like a baby. Trying to stand and walk or even run was impossible. I know this sounds dramatic but that is what mourning can do to you. That is how it affected me. Is this familiar? Trying to see our way clear just to put one foot in front of the other, taking one day at a time.

Death can carry with it a shadow. It can loom in the waiting room or wherever you are when it arrives. This strong feeling or presence does not occur in everyone's experience. The loss of others in my immediate family did not produce this level of awareness. However, the death of my son did. I watched his body fall to the havoc of an invader, having no power of my own to prevent the destruction. A mother's love can be a powerful force but sometimes it is just not enough. As the sun was setting on his life, the darkness in me was setting. I should not have seen it that way. As a believer, I should have seen it as the sun was setting on his life and the light was rising and surrounding him. The light leading to eternal life in Christ Jesus.

How do we deal with shadows? First, we need to understand what a shadow is. Wikipedia says that a shadow is a dark area where light from a light source is blocked by an opaque object. Like with anything else, there are several variations of a shadow's definition. In this context, a shadow is absent of light.

There are many references of the shadow of death in Scripture. In the book of Job several are presented. As Job went through his suffering, and he did suffer, he did not have the view of death as we as Christians know it to be today.

Job 10:21-22 (KJV), "Before I go whence I shall not return, even to the land of darkness and the shadow of death; A land of darkness, as darkness itself; and of the shadow of death, without any order, and where the light is as darkness." Job saw death from an Old Testament view. In his view, death was bleak. He sees it as a land of darkness, the shadow not filtering in light.

While I might have felt the shadow of death, my mind and thoughts engaged, my heart kept true to the reality of what I really believed. Even while my faith was slipping and while I had the 'nevertheless' moment that God's will be done, the Holy Spirit was speaking to my spirit that this shadow was fleeting.

Job's vantage point was narrow of what is to come, namely, God's design for Eternal life through Jesus Christ. "That if thou shalt confess with thy mouth the Lord Jesus, and shalt believe in thine heart that God hath raised him from the dead, thou shalt be saved" (Romans 10:9, KJV). If we are saved, death leads to victory. How? Because of the resurrection. The evidence is the resurrection of Christ Jesus.

During "Mile Marker #1," my faith was tested. I passed the test the first few hours when I kept telling my family that my son would live and not die tonight. I was referencing Psalm 118:17 (KJV), "I shall not die, but live, and declare the works of the Lord." If a family member had asked me the address for the verse, I would not have been able to tell them, but I knew it was in the Word somewhere. I just knew my son would live and have a testimony. He would be a living witness to what God can do: heal. That was my prayer.

What did happen as the hours progressed was my faith failed.

As months went by, a realization was awakened in me that the Lord knew how I would react in those moments. He is all-knowing. What I was feeling did not come as a surprise to Him. Yet, He never left me. He still loved me.

He was with me as I began my walk, crossing the bridge to hope and heaven.

I then reached "Mile Marker #2."

Did your loss carry with it a shadow? How are you dealing with it? Please take time to write the answers to these questions or your own thoughts in the journal pages to follow.

Journal Pages

_____

_____

_____

_____

_____

_____

_____

_____

_____

_____

_____

_____

_____

_____

_____

_____

_____

_____

_____

_____

_____

_____

_____

_____

_____

_____

_____

_____

_____

_____

_____

_____

_____

_____

_____

_____

_____

_____

_____

_____

_____

_____

_____

_____

_____

_____

_____

_____

_____

_____

_____

_____

_____

_____

_____

_____

_____

_____

_____

_____

_____

_____

_____

_____

_____

_____

_____

_____

_____

_____

_____

_____

_____

_____

_____

_____

_____

_____

_____

_____

_____

_____

_____

_____

_____

Mile Marker #2: There is Life After Loss

Can our lives after the loss of a loved one be revived? Can we live after a season of lamenting, suffering in silence and learning to cope with life again? Can we simply pray for a fresh breath of life and will God grant it? There is evidence in God's Word that we can, and He will.

The Old Testament book of Ezekiel provides such evidence in Chapter 37. Ezekiel was of a priestly family and then called to be a prophet when he was exiled along with other Jews to Babylon by Nebuchadnezzar in 597 B. C. A few years later the city of Jerusalem was pillaged, and both the city and the Temple were burned. This man of God was called to minister to the exiles. He walked and ministered in his prophetic calling. His message was one of judgement then a message of hope. The hope was for peace with God during their exile and peace for themselves. There would be no early release from bondage for them. During this time, Ezekiel was told that his wife would die. "….I am about to take away from you the delight of your eyes…" (Ezekiel 24:16, NIV). The Prophet has lost the Temple where he worshipped, the city where he lived, and now the woman he loved, the delight of his eyes. Yet, he still had a message of hope to deliver. One of revival, restoration, and a glorious future as the redeemed people of God.

Starting at Ezekiel 37:1-2, Ezekiel has a vision. The Lord brought him out by the Spirit and set him in the middle of a valley; a valley full of bones and they were very dry.

To paraphrase the text of Ezekiel 37:3, God asks Ezekiel the Prophet, "Can these bones live?" Ezekiel says, "LORD God, only You know." Israel was a divided and dispersed nation; the temple was destroyed, and they were in an impossible position. God tells Ezekiel to prophesy to the bones and say to them,

> "'Dry bones, hear the word of the LORD! This is what the Sovereign LORD says to these bones: I will make breath enter you, and you will come to life. I will attach tendons to you

and make flesh come upon you and cover you
with skin; I will put breath in you, and you
will come to life. Then you will know that I am
the LORD.'"

Ezekiel 37:4b-6, NIV

The Lord God then restores life to the bones. First,
there was a noise, a rattling sound. Then bones came
together each one connecting to the bone where they
belonged. The tendons and flesh grew on the bones,
then skin covered the tendons and flesh that grew on
the bones. There was still one aspect of life missing.
Breath! God tells Ezekiel again to prophesy this time
to the breath and say to it, "This is what the Sovereign
LORD says: Come, breath, from the four winds and
breathe into these slain, that they may live" (Ezekiel
37:9, NIV). God breathed the breath of life into them,
and they lived.

I ask again; Can our lives after the loss of a loved one
be revived? Can we live after a season of lamenting, suffering in silence and learning to cope with life again?
Can we simply pray for a fresh breath of life and will
God grant it?

The answer: Absolutely without a doubt! On a personal level, this needed to reach my thoughts and mind.

Loss can lead us to believe we are defeated. There is a void that will never be filled again. A gap that cannot be mended. As I shared with you earlier, my immediate family has been graduated to glory. While the void will never completely be filled, the death of my son, flesh of my flesh, is an open wound that apparently will not close.

A revival, a renewal is needed, but it is just out of reach for me.

My mind, my thoughts, my spirit were all disconnected, disjointed, scattered aimlessly throughout the months following my sons passing. Only God could put them back in order. We are to be one, mind, body, and spirit. But when one falls out of joint, it can be hard to pick up the pieces, reconnect, breathe again, stand up to the reality of life and move forward. Can these bones live again? God was so patient with me. He sent the breath of His anointing to fall afresh and rest on me. This was the beginning of wholeness, each part of me.

As God told Ezekiel to prophesy to the bones telling them to "hear the Word of the Lord" (Ezekiel 37:4b, NIV), this is a command even for you and me today. We are to "hear the Word of the Lord." Putting all we are going through aside even for a moment to hear what the Word has to say to us.

In this passage God says that the bones shall live. It is a promise, and the Word says in 2 Corinthian 1:20 (KJV), "For all the promises of God in him are yea, and in him Amen, unto the glory of God by us." This means that my return to hope and wholeness, to live again, which is a promise of God through Christ, is already done. His promises are, "Yes," and, "Amen." It does not mean, "Maybe," or "Let us see," or "You can't, "I can't." It means, "He will." The Lord did not want me to stay in the valley of dryness.

This takes me back to what I said to the family when I joined them in the emergency room waiting to hear word of my son's condition. I told them my child would live and not die today. As I am writing this chapter, I recognize part of me died when my son took his last breath. My hope was scattered, parts of me fragmented. However, it was not God's will that I would die on November 1, 2019, along with my son.

I am also taken back to one of my favorite verses in the Bible. It is Lamentations 3:22-24 (KJV), "It is of the LORD's mercies that we are not consumed, because his compassions fail not. They are new every morning: great is thy faithfulness. The LORD is my portion, saith my soul; therefore will I hope in him."

How do we know there is life after loss? Because of the promises of God in His Word and more so for me in this passage in Lamentations. A promise that I have re-cited over and over again, even daily. Yet, I did not draw upon it when I needed it most. Sometimes we find our-selves quoting scripture and not really paying attention to the heart of it. If we did, if I did, then maybe I would have found the comfort I was seeking.

The Book of Lamentations has been attributed to the major prophet Jeremiah. "Lamentations" means to cry aloud. This book is comprised of poems of mourning. Chapter 3 brings to us hope and consolation. Hope is a resounding message. We see God's revealed character, His love, compassion, His grace, and His mercy. King David knew of God's character when he penned Psalm 145:8 (KJV) "The Lord is gracious, and full of compas-sion; slow to anger and of great mercy."

The graciousness of God and His love for us is so clear; "We are not consumed, because his compassions fail not" (Lamentations 3:22, KJV). Whatever we are go-ing through, there is no need for the experience to con-sume us. God's mercies are new every morning. There is hope because every single morning, not one morning is missed regardless of our plight, His mercies are new. When we awake early and hear the birds chirping, see the evidence through our bedroom curtains that the sun is rising we can be assured that His mercies are new. Even on those mornings when raindrops fall against our windows, drop by drop, and our spirit is heavy and getting out of bed is a chore, there is a promise for us, simply, the LORD's mercies will be new on that very day and every day that follows.

God's very nature should have us proclaiming "great is thy faithfulness." When God makes a promise, He holds fast to it. Psalm 91:4 (NLT), "He will cover you with his feathers. He will shelter you with his wings. His faithful promises are your armor and protection." Numbers 23:19 (KJV), "God is not a man, that he should lie; neither the son of man, that he should repent: hath he said, and shall he not do it? or hath he spoken, and shall he not make it good?" God is immutable, which means He is unchangeable. His promises will not fail.

A great hymn of the Church was written based on Lamentations 3:23.

> *Great is thy faithfulness, O God my Father;*
> *there is no shadow of turning with thee;*
> *thou changest not, thy compassions, they fail not;*
> *as thou hast been thou forever wilt be.*
>
> *Great is thy faithfulness!*
> *Great is thy faithfulness!*
> *Morning by morning new mercies I see:*
> *all I have needed thy hand hath provided--*
> *Great is thy faithfulness, Lord, unto me!*

Summer and winter and springtime and harvest,
sun, moon, and stars in their courses above
join with all nature in manifold witness
to thy great faithfulness, mercy, and love.

The Lord is my portion saith my soul so why would I continue to think that my grief was stronger than "my portion." He has always been faithful, merciful, and graciously loving. I hold onto that promise as my steps toward healing and wholeness begins to take shape and in my view is the next "Mile Marker"; "El Roi, The God Who Sees Me."

In the journal pages to follow share your vision and testimony that leads you to know there is life after loss.

Journal Pages

_____

_____

_____

_____

_____

_____

_____

_____

_____

_____

_____

_____

_____

_____

_____

_____

_____

_____

_____

_____

_____

_____

_____

_____

_____

_____

_____

_____

_____

_____

_____

_____

_____

_____

_____

_____

_____

_____

_____

_____

_____

_____

_____

_____

_____

_____

_____

_____

_____

_____

_____

_____

_____

_____

_____

_____

_____

_____

_____

_____

_____

_____

_____

_____

_____

_____

_____

_____

_____

_____

_____

_____

_____

_____

_____

_____

_____

_____

_____

_____

_____

_____

_____

Mile Marker #3: El Roi, The God Who Sees Me

There are many names of God, but one that I fell in love with long before my great sadness is El Roi. I have called on this name of God many times over the years. How extraordinary to have a God who sees me for who I am and what I am experiencing. This name is so personal. He sees me! Me! Throughout the entire time my son struggled for life then succumbed to death, God never took His eyes off me. He never took His eyes off my son. He was waiting for the call of my child's name by the angels to enter eternity.

God is omniscient, all-knowing; He is omnipresent, He is present everywhere at the same time. When no one else could possibly know exactly how I was feeling, the God who sees did. 1 Peter 3:12 (NIV) says, "For the eyes of the Lord are on the righteous." God was moved with compassion even when I was searching for Him. He was there and saw me clearly. 2 Chronicles 16:9 (NLT), "The eyes of the Lord search the whole earth in order to strengthen those who hearts are fully committed to him." Psalm 34:15, 17, & 18 (NLT):

> The eyes of the LORD watch over those who do right;
> his ears are open to their cries for help.
> The LORD hears his people when they call to him
>   for help.
> He rescues them from all their troubles.
> The LORD is close to the brokenhearted;
> he rescues those whose spirits are crushed.

When my faith dwindled, when I questioned Him, when I felt lost, alone, and sad, He saw me. Why would I ever doubt Him?

The Word in Matthew 6:26 says that the Lord takes care of the fowls of the air. In the treasure chest of my favorite hymns is "His Eye is on the Sparrow." One verse says, "for His eye is on the Sparrow and I know He watches me." I sing the song in church with heartfelt fervency, hands raised toward heaven in praise. He watches me. Matthew 10:30 is clear that God knows the number of the very hairs on our head.

As we cross the bridge to hope and heaven, each "Mile Marker" takes us closer to the towers on the bridge. The tower that bears the strain, the tension, and the weight of our experience. As I said in an earlier chapter, the pure length of a suspension bridge means many forces are at work to secure it and to transfer the weight to a stronger area that can handle the pressure. The strong tower of the God that sees us, El Roi.

This name of God, El Roi, is found only in Genesis. That makes the name even more special, precious, and revealing.

Please step into the book of Genesis with me where we find Hagar, a bondservant and mother. Who was this woman who met God in the desert?

It is suspected that we first meet Hagar, although not named, in Genesis 12:16. The account of Abram and Sarai is rich with the blessings and promises of God. God told Abram to get out of his country, leaving behind his kindred to travel to the place that God showed him. Abram trusted God and was obedient. He followed God's direction, taking his wife Sarai with him, as well as others, and his substance. They journeyed to Canaan. There was a famine in the land, so they went down to Egypt. You can read this account in Genesis 12:10–20. God had to step into a situation that Abram had caused.

They had to leave Egypt to return to Canaan. Abram had gained livestock, menservants, and maidservants. It is thought that Hagar was in that number, taken from the homeland where she lived. Being a slave of Abram and Sarai, Hagar had no say in things to come and no power to step away.

As I have a story and you have a story, Hagar has a story as well. You will find hers in Genesis 12:10-20; 16:1-16; 21:8-21.

Hagar's story unfolds and intersects with Sarai and Abram. A decision was made for Hagar, she found herself in a place not of her own choosing. How did she get there, how does she find a way out? These scriptures in Genesis involves three people. Abram who was promised an heir by God in Genesis 15:4, and Sarai, his wife who knew of the promise, yet believed at her age she could not bear a child. Sarai took the situation into her own hands rather than waiting on the promise of God. She gave Hagar, her handmaid, to Abram as a wife (Genesis 16:3) to bear an offspring. She would be the surrogate mother. Hagar conceived. There then arose a rift between the two women. Hagar became puffed and condescending during her pregnancy toward Sarai and Sarai dealt with her cruelly with jealousy. Sarai relegated her back to the master and servant relationship. This was blessed by Abram who told Sarai to do with Hagar as she pleased. Hagar fled to the wilderness to escape.

The angel of the Lord found Hagar in the wilderness. This angel of the Lord was a self-manifestation of God, a theophany. The angel spoke as God. He asked Hagar, "Where did you come from and where are you going?" (Genesis 16:8, NLT). Her response was that she fled from her mistress Sarai. The angel of the Lord told her to return to Sarai and submit herself under her hands. The angel went further with a promise, "I will multiply thy seed exceedingly" (Genesis 16:10, KJV). Then He gave a prophetic declaration of a son and gave the son a name along with a description of his character. The Lord heard her distress.

Here in the wilderness Hagar met God, El Roi, "Thou God seest me" (Genesis 16:13, KJV). Hagar flees from her circumstance only to meet El Roi. She was never alone; God knew her circumstances. He was the God of Psalm 46:1 (KJV), "God is our refuge and strength, a very present help in trouble."

El Roi, the God that sees me! How precious is that revelation. All His promises are in effect because He knows. Psalm 139:2 (KJV), "Thou knowest my downsitting and mine uprising, thou understandest my thought afar off."

Hagar was asked a question in Genesis 16:8 (NLT). Contemplate this for a moment. What if we are asked that question today what would be our response? "Where have we come from and where are we going?" Looking through the rear-view mirror from whence I came, I suppose I would answer, "Lord, I am coming from the seashore of grief. The waves beating against the shoreline, each wave bringing with it hurt, heart- ache, tears."

Where am I going? What lies ahead? I may not have a clear picture right now but what I do know, I do not want to relive my experience like I do now almost daily, as though it just happened yesterday. I do not want to stay where I am now. I want the autonomy, the strength, the guidance, and support of the Lord to move forward. Proverbs 3:5-6 (KJV), "Trust in the LORD with all thine heart; and lean not unto thine own understanding. In all thy ways acknowledge him, and he shall direct thy paths."

In Hagar's situation, it was necessary that she go back. This same God who saw her circumstance and gave her guidance, is the same God that sees us in ours. While they differ, I can imagine He would say to us, my child "weeping may endure for a night, but joy cometh in the morning" (Psalm 30:5, KJV).

Hagar met El Roi in the wilderness, and He saw her plight. I know that He sees me, sees you, and where we are now. He gave Hagar promises of a future and El Roi, gives us promises for our life in His Word.

Early in this book I referenced "the widow of Nain" from Luke Chapter 7. She was a mother whose only son died, and she was a widow. I said she would be referenced again as her story did not end with her putting one foot in front of the other as her son's body was being carried. In Luke 7:13 (KJV), the Lord Jesus saw her. He had compassion on her and said unto her, "Weep not."

There is yet other evidence that He sees us in the book of Luke 13:10-13. Jesus saw a woman in the synagogue service while He was teaching. She had a spirit of infirmity eighteen years. She was bent over and could not straighten up. Jesus saw her, called her forward, and said to her, "Woman thou art loosed from thine infirmity" (Luke 13:12, KJV). Then He laid hands on her and she was healed.

Jesus saw this woman. She did not scream out to Him, neither did she disrupt the service. He saw her, called her to Him, laid hands on her, and she was healed.

Hebrews 13:8 (KJV) states that "Jesus Christ the same yesterday, and to day, and for ever (sic.)." If the eyes of the Lord saw Hagar, the widow of Nain, the woman in the church service and others who could testify in the Bible, He surely and certainly sees us.

Some verses are worth repeating:

1 Peter 3:12 (NIV), "The eyes of the Lord are on the righteous." 2 Chronicles 16:9 (NLT), "The eyes of the Lord search the whole earth in order to strengthen those who hearts are fully committed to him" (Psalm 34:15, 17, & 18, NLT).

> *The eyes of the LORD watch over those who do right;*
> *his ears are open to their cries for help.*
> *The LORD hears his people when they call to him*
>   *for help.*
> *He rescues them from all their troubles.*
> *The LORD is close to the brokenhearted;*
> *he rescues those whose spirits are crushed.*

When God sees you and me, He sees us through His eyes of love, compassion, and hope. He will guide us, direct us, and allow us to rest in green pastures beside the still waters as He restores our soul. Crossing the bridge to hope and heaven, I have now reached "Mile Marker #4."

Describe your encounter with "El Roi, the God Who Sees You" as you journal.

Journal Pages

_____

_____

_____

_____

_____

_____

_____

_____

_____

_____

_____

_____

_____

_____

_____

_____

_____

_____

_____

_____

_____

_____

_____

_____

_____

_____

_____

_____

_____

_____

_____

_____

_____

_____

_____

_____

_____

_____

_____

_____

_____

_____

_____

_____

_____

_____

_____

_____

_____

_____

_____

_____

_____

_____

_____

_____

_____

_____

_____

_____

_____

_____

_____

_____

_____

_____

_____

Mile Marker #4: He Restoreth My Soul

Anger! Have you experienced anger during your grief journey? To be perfectly honest, I had not experienced this emotion. Questioning God? Yes. Tolerating others? Yes. Anger toward the loved ones I lost? Not really. However, it has now manifested itself. I found myself taking anger out on others because of a situation or circumstance that did not meet my immediate need. Angry because the loved one was not here to celebrate an important milestone in my life or was not by my side when I needed comforting. I needed deliverance!

There could be a multitude of reasons that can bring on this emotion. Some justified, but most often unjustified. An apology may be necessary, but we just do not feel up to giving it. *Why can't they understand what we are feeling and what we are going through?* A prayer is in order when these feelings arise.

> "Lord, please forgive me for this moment of anger in all forms against another. May this mood and ugly spirit leave me immediately. Create in me a clean heart, O God; and renew a right spirit within me. I pray that your holy presence will engulf me and fill me until there is no more room for anger. In Jesus' name I pray. Amen."

Emotions! Our emotions can ride the roller coaster within and appear outwardly, to those who know us, that we are irrational or contentious. If these are not descriptive then maybe we are seen as everything is all right. In that case, we wear our masks tightly fitted. Internally boiling up, but externally all is well. Will we ever rid ourselves of the ups and downs of emotions that are brought on because of our loss? The question and remedy may be found in Psalms 42:11 (NIV), "Why, my soul, are you downcast? Why so disturbed within me? Put your hope in God, for I will yet praise him, my Savior and my God."

We cannot overlook our emotions because they were brought on by reality. Plain and simple, the loss. But we can seek solace in the Word of God.

Psalm 23 is so healing for us as we grieve and move from those volatile or unfeeling emotions toward wholeness and healing. Case in point, Psalm 23:2-3a (KJV) reads: "He maketh me to lie down in green pastures: he leadeth me beside the still waters. He restoreth my soul."

The initial verses of this Psalm can bring calm to the soul. A quiet calmness. Here is life under a divine shepherd caring for His lamb. There is love in this image and compassion as the shepherd leads His flock. David wrote the 23rd Psalm. He wrote it from a place of experience, as early in his life as a shepherd child tending his father's sheep.

> The Lord is my Shepherd; I shall not want. He maketh me to lie down in green pastures: he leadeth me beside the still waters: He restoreth my soul.
>
> Psalm 23:1-3a (KJV)

These first three verses infiltrate my heart and soul. The Lord's presence is with us. This is the God that reveals Himself to provide everything we need which includes care, comfort, and love. He has also revealed Himself in His Son, Jesus Christ, who proclaimed, "I am the Good Shepherd; I know my sheep and my sheep know me – just as the Father knows me and I know the Father – and I lay down my life for the sheep" (John 10:14-15, NIV). He has done just that.

These verses not only suggest that the shepherd is our provider, the shepherd is guiding us to rest and promotes a quiet spirit within us. Green pastures: grass, lush with texture and color, where rest can be found. His gentleness is so evident and needed when we find ourselves weary and heavy laden.

Psalm 23, within the second verse He consoles us by saying, "He leads us beside the still waters." There is no turbulence or raging streams. Peace, just as when Jesus calmed the raging sea, commanding, "Peace, be still" (Mark 4:39, KJV). Just as He can calm and stabilize our multitude of emotions that we experience.

Peace. A melody which soothes and dries our tears. May I suggest you close your eyes and visualize. Let the image rise before you. What do you see?

There is a picture on another wall in my house. It brings me such peace just gazing upon it. There is a young woman sitting at the foot of steps which lead to a house. The woman is meditating in an atmosphere of peace. The walkway runs alongside a still body of water. Separating this body of water, is a patch of lush green grass. Psalm 145:5 (NKJV) is the quote at the top of the picture, "I will meditate on the glorious splendor of Your majesty, And on Your wondrous works."

There are occasions when we need moments of stillness; mediating, praying, and basking in the goodness of the Lord. A time of refreshing. If we are still and pray as the Holy Spirit leads, maybe, we will be open enough to hear from God. Even the Word in Psalm 46:10 (NKJV) reminds us to "Be still, and know that I *am* God."

Psalm 77:1-7 (NIV),

> I cried out to God for help; I cried out to God to hear me. When I was in distress, I sought the Lord; at night I stretched out untiring hands, and I would not be comforted. I remembered you, God, and I groaned; I meditated, and my spirit grew faint. You kept my eyes from closing; I was too troubled to speak. I thought about the former days, the years of long ago; I remembered my songs in the night. My heart meditated and my spirit asked: "Will the Lord reject forever? Will he never show his favor again?"

We are seekers of peace, internal and external, as we deal with loss. I know you agree that we cannot put a price on a night's peaceful sleep as it is priceless.

Digging deep again into my treasure chest of hymns is a song of which the stanzas are so appropriate, "Blessed Quietness."

> *Joys are flowing like a river*
> *Since the Comforter has come;*
> *He abides with us forever,*
> *Makes the trusting heart His home.*
> *Blessed quietness, holy quietness*
> *What assurance in my soul!*
> *On the stormy sea*
> *He speaks peace to me*
> *How the billows cease to roll!*

The Psalmist then pens verse 3, "He restoreth my soul" (KJV). This is a "Mile Marker" of promise. Our soul is strengthened and repaired. Our soul is alive with God. God's grace can restore and repair our soul.

A dictionary definition of restoration is to bring back, reinstate, return, repair to its original condition.

As I press through "Mile Marker #4," my pressing fluctuates between lamenting and praise. The heaviness of mourning and grief is just starting to subside.

The Lord is restoring my soul.

Through His Word, "The law of the LORD is perfect, refreshing the soul. The statutes of the LORD are trust-worthy, making wise the simple" (Psalm 19:7, NIV).

Through praise we may "praise the LORD, my soul; all my inmost being, praise his holy name" (Psalm 103:1, NIV).

Through rest "Come to me, all you who are weary and burdened, and I will give you rest. Take my yoke upon you and learn from me, for I am gentle and humble in heart, and you will find rest for your souls" (Matthew 11:28-29, NIV).

While still not far away from deep hurt and loss, salvation creeps through the curtains with trust by its side. I am certain God will restore and refresh to the extent that I can put down the anchor of this sinking ship. I am halfway to crossing the bridge to hope and heaven.

Savior of my restoration, repairing of my soul is the Lord, my shepherd—the God of the Old Testament. God's Son of the New Testament and the Holy Spirit are my comforters. Did I forget the goodness of God? Maybe temporarily. When He restores our soul, He restores our confidence giving us a time of refreshing. He is leading us out of the desert and wilderness to a place of beauty again. He is taking my hands and leading me to the springs of living water. I have been carried when I could not walk. Early on, I cried out for help, questioning God why my son died while I yet lived. Grief can momentarily cloud our senses pulling us away sending our sensibilities on a vacation. But just as Psalm 23:3a (KJV) states, "He restoreth my soul."

I stayed at "Mile Marker #4" for a long time because I needed to begin to feel whole again. We quoted the 23rd Psalm at the bedside during the last moments of my son's life on earth. As a child, he learned it in Sunday school so I knew it would bring him comfort. This loss touched my very soul. Grief can reach down into our inner most soul and take up residence. But we know the Lord our shepherd can restore and repair. Please read the whole Psalm. It starts with provision, promotes quietness, peace, calmness then power and a promise. The last verse reflects sunshine into eternity.

It has now brought me comfort as it will you.

> The Lord is my Shepherd; I shall not want.
> He maketh me to lie down in green pastures:
> he leadeth me beside the still waters:
> He restoreth my soul.
>
> Psalm 23:1-3a (KJV)

I open the lid of hymns in my treasure chest again and there are two more I want to share with you while still at this "Mile Marker." It has become part of my testimony and hopefully yours, too. "It is Well with My Soul"

When peace, like a river, attendeth my way,
When sorrows like sea – billows roll;
Whatever my lot, Thou hast taught me to say,
It is well, it is well with my soul.

And here is a song of praise.

"How Great Thou Art"

Then sings my soul, my Savior God, to Thee;
How great Thou art, how great Thou art!
Then sings my soul, my Savior God, to Thee;
How great Thou art, how great Thou Art!

The clouds are lifting as I touch the starting line of "Mile Marker #5."

Journal Pages

_____

_____

_____

_____

_____

_____

_____

_____

_____

_____

_____

_____

_____

_____

_____

_____

_____

_____

_____

_____

_____

_____

_____

_____

_____

_____

_____

_____

_____

_____

_____

_____

_____

_____

_____

_____

_____

_____

_____

_____

_____

_____

_____

_____

_____

_____

_____

_____

_____

_____

_____

_____

_____

_____

_____

_____

_____

_____

_____

_____

_____

_____

_____

_____

_____

_____

_____

_____

_____

_____

_____

_____

_____

_____

_____

_____

_____

_____

_____

_____

_____

_____

_____

Mile Marker #5: Out of the Fog: A Visit with Job

As I got closer to "Mile Marker #6," a chapter of hope, the fog began to lift. I start to see my way out of the intensity of mourning, hurt, and lament.

Advancing through the fog, I look through the rearview mirror and there appears Job again, a man who endured great loss and pain. In the Word of God, the book of Job, chapter by chapter we stand outside looking in on Job's journey from loss to wholeness and restoration. Just as others looked at me, at you, as they stood outside the looking glass with only a glimpse of our experiences. You cannot really identify unless you have lost someone so precious in your life.

Believing there would be a glimmer of light and wholeness when the fog began to lift, Job Chapter 38 came to the forefront of my memory. I often read this chapter to remind me of who God is and His sovereignty. While I have read through the book of Job, it is the Lord's speeches directed at Job, challenging him, that puts me in my place, a place of humility.

If you have not read the book of Job, let me give you a short overview.

Job was stricken with disease, sore boils from the sole of his feet to his crown. He lost his livestock, his servants died, more impactful, he experienced the death of his children. Job had friends who could have been better friends and a wife—well, you will just have to read for yourself (Job 2:9). Just keep in mind, though, that she encountered loss as well.

I use Job as a point of reference for this chapter because he went through so much, more than any of us, although I cannot speak for you. In Job's case there was a reason for his suffering of which he was not made aware. There was a conversation in Heaven that did not include Job. Read Job Chapters 1 and 2.

In my case, the death of my only child, on an appointed day in November 2019, is a mystery. One that only the Lord can provide insight and clarity if He chooses to do so on this side of Heaven. I needed to remember and recite over and over that my God is sovereign. He is in control. God know all things, omniscience, and He is everywhere, omnipresent, God is all powerful, omnipotent. As I have said before, in my heart of hearts, I know without a shadow of doubt that my God loves me and works on my behalf. That goes for you, too. Job, just like some of us, may have wished he would not have lived (Job 6:8-9). His hope was dissolving (Job 10:20-22). However, in spite of all he was going through, Job trusted God (Job 13:15, 16:19, 23:10).

Moving through the fog with anticipation of a clearing on the horizon, trust is the key.

Job wanted answers just like I did, more than likely you, too, and still do. He asked, "But where shall wisdom be found? and where is the place of understanding?" (Job 28:12, KJV). While in the abyss of desolation, what Job got was a direct communication from a sovereign God. God, the supreme ruler who is in control, out of a whirlwind began asking Job a series of questions.

When I read this chapter again, I became so humble. In my face was a reminder of who God was, is, and will always be. Yes, all these months, like a boat rocking in the water, my faith rocked, too. It is a wonder I was not seasick. Yes, I asked God on numerous occasions why He did not heal my child. Where was He when I needed

Him? Yet I knew in my heart of hearts and my soul that He never left. Being perfectly honest, I knew that my sovereign God did not have to answer me. The problem was that my mind was not in sync. Was I being tested? Interesting thought.

Here is Job Chapter 38 (NLT). Please read it and put your thoughts in the journal pages. Take another look at your relationship with the Lord, knowing that His love is bountiful and everlasting.

The LORD Challenges Job

Then the LORD answered Job from the
    whirlwind:
Who is this that questions my wisdom
with such ignorant words?
Brace yourself like a man,
because I have some questions for you,
and you must answer them.

Where were you when I laid the foundations
    of the earth?
Tell me, if you know so much.
Who determined its dimensions
and stretched out the surveying line?
What supports its foundations,
and who laid its cornerstone

as the morning stars sang together
and all the angels shouted for joy?

Who kept the sea inside its boundaries
as it burst from the womb,
and as I clothed it with clouds
and wrapped it in thick darkness?
For I locked it behind barred gates,
limiting its shores.
I said, "This far and no farther will you come.
Here your proud waves must stop!"

Have you ever commanded the morning to
    appear
and caused the dawn to rise in the east?

Have you explored the springs from which the
    seas come?
Have you explored their depths?
Do you know where the gates of death are
    located?
Have you seen the gates of utter gloom?
Do you realize the extent of the earth?
Tell me about it if you know!
Where does light come from,
and where does darkness go?
Can you take each to its home?
Do you know how to get there?

But of course you know all this!
For you were born before it was all created,
and you are so very experienced!
Have you visited the storehouses of the snow
or seen the storehouses of hail?
(I have reserved them as weapons for the time
    of trouble,
for the day of battle and war.)
Where is the path to the source of light?
Where is the home of the east wind?
Who created a channel for the torrents of
    rain?
Who laid out the path for the lightning?
Who makes the rain fall on barren land,
in a desert where no one lives?
Who sends rain to satisfy the parched ground
and make the tender grass spring up?
Does the rain have a father?
Who gives birth to the dew?
Who is the mother of the ice?
Who gives birth to the frost from the heavens?
For the water turns to ice as hard as rock,
and the surface of the water freezes.
Can you direct the movement of the stars—
binding the cluster of the Pleiades
or loosening the cords of Orion?
Can you direct the constellations through the
    seasons

or guide the Bear with her cubs across the
   heavens?
Do you know the laws of the universe?
Can you use them to regulate the earth?
Can you shout to the clouds
and make it rain?
Can you make lightning appear
and cause it to strike as you direct?
Who gives intuition to the heart
and instinct to the mind?
Who is wise enough to count all the clouds?
Who can tilt the water jars of heaven
when the parched ground is dry
and the soil has hardened into clods?
Can you stalk prey for a lioness
and satisfy the young lions' appetites
as they lie in their dens
or crouch in the thicket?
Who provides food for the ravens
when their young cry out to God
and wander about in hunger?

God's speech does not end here. Read Chapters 39,
40 and 41.

In chapter 42 verse 1-5 we read Job's response:

Then Job replied to the LORD:

I know that you can do anything,
and no one can stop you.
You asked, "Who is this that questions my
wisdom with such ignorance?"
It is I—and I was talking about things I knew
nothing about,
things far too wonderful for me.
You said, "Listen and I will speak!
I have some questions for you,
and you must answer them."
I had only heard about you before,
but now I have seen you with my own eyes.

Reading Job's response, it seems to have come down to him realizing his own unfamiliarity of God. However, Job himself says that through this circumstance, he has seen God and he responds in repentance.

Trust is the turning point for Job and trust is the same defining moment for us. We see the omni attributes of God our creator; all powerful, all knowing, ever present. There is no answer that we can demand from Him. Who are we that we could ever think or possibly imagine that we can demand answers from the sovereign God? Jude 1:25 (NLT), "All glory to him who alone is God, our Savior through Jesus Christ our Lord. All glory, majesty, power, and authority are his before all time, and in the present, and beyond all time! Amen."

If the Lord chooses to reveal answers, then we get more than we ought to have or deserve. Do you know what is so great? Despite Job's anger, frustration, moments of lamenting, the Lord still loved him and accepted him. Then the splendor appears, God blesses Job 42:12a (NIV) "The Lord blessed the latter part of Job's life more than the former part."

Know this my fellow traveler of this journey, as we cross the bridge to hope and heaven, we cannot erase our loss whomever it is or whatever it is. The hole in our hearts may begin to heal or it can be permanent but either way we must trust that it will hurt less as time passes.

My loss may not have been as catastrophic as Job's loss, but to each of us, our individual loss is great and unique and had a definite impact on our lives.

Job, on one hand, wanted God to appear and explain Himself, so that he could rationalize what was happening to him. However, on the other hand there was a certainty of Job, one of which we can testify. "For I know that my redeemer liveth, and that he shall stand at the latter day upon the earth." (Job 19:25, KJV)

In the chapter "Mile Marker #3", we see that Hagar experienced El Roi, the "God who sees me." Just listen to what Job proclaims in the last chapter. "My ears had heard of you but now my eyes have seen you." (Job 42:5 NIV)

Job lost all his children but his faith in God was un-daunted (Job 1:21). Divine providence is realized and Job refused to give up his faith. Any doubt he had was swallowed up by his faith in the living God. What a testimony for us to follow suit.

Closing this "Mile Marker" with reference again to the analogy of a suspension bridge: when crossing a bridge, in fog, the density can be so thick and heavy, surrounding the very road traveled. Visibility can also be zero initially. Your pace slows because you cannot see what is ahead. It could be so dense that you may have to pull over. Lights may help or not but most often they are on. The instrument panel on your dashboard, if driving a car, may become vital. Such as the headlights, the speedometer, the GPS, windshield wipers, to name a few. There may be an element of fear and uncertainty because you do not want to hit an obstacle or a barrier. If the sun is shining above the clouds as you move forward, a beam of sunlight may start to shine through. If positioned exactly right, the beam may flow through the tower on the bridge offering you a spectacle of shear illumination and beauty. Also, a clearing to see your way through.

As I make my way through the fog, I begin to use all the instruments that the Lord has given me on my spiritual dashboard. The headlights can illuminate the road and guide my path just like the Word of God. Psalm 119:105 (KJV) "Thy word is a lamp unto my feet, and a light unto my path." The speedometer can gauge if I am moving too fast through the fog because I just want to get out of this state of sorrow more quickly. It can gauge if I am moving too slow because I have become accustomed to sorrow and in that state of mind, I may linger too long. My spiritual GPS can make sure I am heading in the right direction. In Psalm 32:8 (CSB), "I will instruct you and show you the way to go; with My eye on you, I will give counsel." My spiritual windshield wipers will keep my tears at bay, so I am able to see ahead, to see the tower just ahead, the strong tower through the denseness. Lastly, the gas gauge represents not running out of strength because I know I can ask the Holy Spirit for a fresh infilling.

As I have written before, and needs to be repeated as a reminder for us as we move through the fog of sorrow,

> If the sun is shining above the clouds as you move forward, a beam of sunlight may start to shine through. If positioned exactly right, the beam may flow through the tower on the bridge offering you a spectacle of shear illu-

mination and beauty. Also a clearing to see your way through.

The clearing is from our God, the strong tower, who has given us His Word, the Bible, as our guide, our instruction, our salvation for healing. That is what we need to keep moving forward, crossing the bridge to hope and heaven. Please write in your journal pages of your journey through the fog of grief and what you glean from Job's story.

Carry with you God's majesty and mystery as we embark on "Mile Marker #6."

Journal Pages

_____

_____

_____

_____

_____

_____

_____

_____

_____

_____

_____

_____

_____

_____

_____

_____

_____

_____

_____

_____

_____

_____

_____

_____

_____

_____

_____

_____

_____

_____

_____

_____

_____

_____

_____

_____

_____

_____

_____

_____

_____

_____

_____

_____

_____

_____

_____

_____

_____

_____

_____

_____

_____

_____

_____

_____

_____

_____

_____

_____

_____

_____

_____

_____

_____

_____

_____

_____

_____

_____

_____

_____

_____

_____

_____

_____

_____

_____

_____

_____

_____

_____

_____

_____

Mile Marker #6: Hope—The Exchange

Hope! In Lamentations 3, the Prophet Jeremiah, often called the 'weeping prophet,' remembered his experience, misery, gloom and discouragement, the back and forth between unbelief and faith. Then his soul in remembrance causes the prophet to be humbled and recollect that he has "hope" in the God he serves. "The LORD is my portion, saith my soul; therefore will I hope in him" (Lamentations 3:24 KJV).

Hope! It may not shine bright as we go through the minutes, hours, days, and months of heartache, but if you know Jesus Christ as Savior and Lord, hope never leaves your soul.

Crossing the bridge to hope and heaven, I had no idea when I would reach the "Mile Marker" of hope in my journey. It has taken me quite some time to get to this point, almost two years, but it seems I now have arrived.

I was looking forward to feeling normal. A new normal, of course, since life is not exactly the same because of the void left by loss. I can now, in total honesty and freedom, give God the praise and the glory He most certainly deserves for His love, His help, His faithfulness. His steadiness journeyed with me through difficult times. Even now as I enter this season of hope. When the intensity of grief and pain consumed me, He was there. When the flood of tears dripped heavily, He stored them in His bottle and recorded each one in his book (Psalm 56:8). He promised never to leave me, and He fulfilled that promise. Hope!

I have finally reached the "Mile Marker" of hope! To God be the glory! I have spent most of my life knowing the hope that comes with the saving grace of our Lord and Savior, Jesus Christ. I have read it, studied it, sang it, walked it, and testified about it. It has been available to me and to you. Hope!

My son was saved, and I knew it unequivocally. As his body failed and the end of his life was becoming a reality, I had to remember, through the cloudiness that engulfed me by his bedside, that he made an exchange when he accepted Jesus Christ as his personal Savior. An exchange for an inheritance. The inheritance of eternal life. He had that blessed hope and knew victory before he collapsed.

It was me that encountered hopelessness as he faded away. I should have focused on the reality of his salvation and the hope he had that when he took his last breath he would be present with the Lord. Instead, I took my eyes off of my son's salvation and his entrance through time and space to be present for eternity with Jesus Christ. I focused on what my eyes saw those many hours in the hospital, his heart stopping and the resuscitations, the tubes attached, and the sound of the life sustaining machines. I focused on my experience, my hurt, my gut-wrenching loss, and my sorrow. This, among other reactions, is normal because we are yet in the flesh. But there was no joy and celebration in my spirit that my child had arrived. He was in the presence of the Lord. Every word imparted in him since his childhood led him to be ready when death appeared at his doorstep. He was prepared, but I was not prepared. The celebration within me has taken a long time to materialize.

As I have said earlier in this book, I did not die physically on the day my child died. So still alive, I should have held on to the Word, the verses that would sustain me as the days passed, such as the second part of John 10:10 (KJV) spoken by Jesus, "I am come that they might have life, and that they might have it more abundantly." That was a promise for me and a promise for you. Life goes on and it can be lived abundantly. We cannot stay and linger for long in the stage of sorrow for the loss we encountered. Jesus has given us abundant life yet to come. There is a future for us and a purpose.

This verse of exchange is for you and me as we journey crossing the bridge to hope and heaven. Isaiah 61:3 is for such a time as this. It offers us hope. It offers us an exchange for our pain, our grief, the weight of our wounds and our despair. It offers us beauty, joy, restoration of our praise, and spiritual health deeply rooted.

All this time I could not turn my hurt and grief over the Lord in my own power. If I could, I would have done it already. How many times have we taken our heartaches and what we are feeling presently to the altar and took it back with us when our prayer ended? Once off our knees, grief can continue to send us "fiery darts" one by one. We have to give it all over to Christ. We needed then and now the help of the Holy Ghost. "Now the God of hope fill you with all joy and peace in believing, that ye may abound in hope, through the power of the Holy Ghost" (Romans 15:13, KJV).

The exchange in Isaiah 61:3 (KJV),

To appoint unto them that mourn in Zion, to give unto them beauty for ashes, the oil of joy for mourning, the garment of praise for the spirit of heaviness; that they might be called trees of righteousness, the planting of the LORD, that he might be glorified.

The Word of God in the Old Testament is applicable to us even in this day and time. This verse in Isaiah speaks to those who mourn, it speaks to us offering hope. God is merciful, and through His power we can find ourselves transitioning and moving forward with our lives. He gives us this so that He may be glorified. That means He gets the glory for these blessings. We open our mouths and proclaim who He is. I anticipate you are encouraged by this verse as I have been.

Isaiah 61:3 offers us a replacement for the emotions, the despair, depression, anxiety, and even fear of what the future holds. Everything that has consumed us from the onset. There are scriptures that relate to ashes as an expression of sorrow and grief.

Beauty! If we give the Lord what lies in our ashes, our deep and penetrating burden of sorrow, our guilt and regret, He can and will give us in return the beauty of His grace, mercy, and peace. We must open ourselves up and be willing to be released from captivity and accept our cup being filled to the brim with the beauty of His presence and His holiness.

Joy! An emotion we may not have felt in some time. If we did, it may have been fleeting. In exchange for our mourning, Isaiah 61:3 says we will receive the oil of joy. The Lord knows that we need an anointing to help us move forward and live a full life despite our circumstances. Joy and contentment can be found when the center of our attention is on the Lord. David understood this when he wrote Psalm 16:8-9 (KJV): "I have set the Lord always before me: because he is at my right hand, I shall not be moved. Therefore my heart is glad, and my glory rejoiceth: my flesh also shall rest in hope." The joy that comes in the morning is in the saving grace of Jesus Christ and the presence of the Holy Spirit that lives within us. How glorious it is to receive the anointing of joy that causes our cup to overflow.

Praise! The garment of praise for the spirit of heaviness. The spirit of heaviness seems to arrive and infiltrate our mind, body and spirit when loss occurs. It lingers and weighs on us. It depends on each individual how long it lasts. The heaviness brings with it so many emotions and can stunt and cripple our movements. Daily activities that used to be a breeze to get through, then becomes cumbersome. It can even reach our spirituality. So heavy that when you look at your reflection in the mirror, you question if it is really you who you see.

This exchange gives us the power to rise up from the ashes. We can see ourselves clear of debilitating mourning and experience the relief from the weight of all we have endured. Like a Phoenix, we can soar, become stronger again, and see the future and purpose for our lives. Swapping the stages of grief for a garment of praise.

I must be truthful; the swap has not been immediate for me. It has been a process. I fight the spirit of heaviness when it comes upon me with the weapon that the Lord has given me. That being praise. Praising the Lord Jesus for deliverance. Worshipping Him for who He is. Praising Him with a loud voice to overtake the other voices. Praising Him each morning for "This is the day which the LORD hath made; we will rejoice and be glad in it" (Psalm 118:24, KJV). Praising Him with thankfulness for His Word that offers hope for the sunlit days to come. Thanking Him for the beauty restored, the joy in my heart, the praise that easily rolls off my lips now and the song that resonates in my spirit. "In every thing give thanks: for this is the will of God in Christ Jesus concerning you" (1 Thessalonians 5:18, KJV). Praising God until our cup tips over.

We are to stand firm regardless of our circumstance, regardless of the unexpected twist and turns of life, grounded, and rooted in Christ Jesus. Our walk is to be pleasing in the sight of the Lord. Our faith should be solid, our witness, testimony, and the hope within us ready to share with others. "But sanctify the Lord God in your hearts: and be ready always to give an answer to every man that asketh you a reason of the hope that is in you with meekness and fear" (1 Peter 3:15, KJV).

Reaching the "Mile Marker" of hope swings the door open for a new season in our lives. If you recently lost a loved one you will not be at this point of your journey. There will, however, come a time that you begin to heal and a new season, one of hope for the future awaits you. If you have walked the walk of brokenness and sorrow for an extended time, remember "weeping may endure for a night, but joy cometh in the morning" (Psalm 30:5b, KJV).

As we reach the last mile marker, crossing the bridge to hope and heaven, keep this thought in mind. We see death as a period when in fact it is a comma.

"We are confident, I say, and willing rather to be absent from the body, and to be present with the Lord" (2 Corinthians 5:8, KJV).

The hope of the resurrection is talked about in 1Thessalonians 4:13-18 (KJV),

> But I would not have you to be ignorant, brethren, concerning them which are asleep, that ye sorrow not, even as others which have no hope. For if we believe that Jesus died and rose again, even so them also which sleep in Jesus will God bring with him. For this we say unto you by the word of the Lord, that we which are alive and remain unto the coming of the Lord shall not prevent them which are asleep. For the Lord himself shall descend from heaven with a shout, with the voice of the archangel, and with the trump of God: and the dead in Christ shall rise first: Then we which are alive and remain shall be caught up together with them in the clouds, to meet the Lord in the air: and so shall we ever be with the Lord. Wherefore comfort one another with these words.

In the journal pages that follow I encourage you to write about the hope in your spirit and the exchange that you know Jesus Christ has waiting for you.

Journal Pages

_____

_____

_____

_____

_____

_____

_____

_____

_____

_____

_____

_____

_____

_____

_____

_____

_____

_____

_____

_____

_____

_____

_____

_____

_____

_____

_____

_____

_____

_____

_____

_____

_____

_____

_____

_____

_____

_____

_____

_____

_____

_____

_____

_____

_____

_____

_____

_____

_____

_____

_____

_____

_____

_____

_____

_____

_____

_____

_____

_____

_____

_____

_____

_____

_____

_____

_____

_____

Mile Marker #7: Destination Heaven—The Resurrection

This "Mile Marker" is a short distance to travel. No need to dwell or slow up. The destination is within view. I can feel the divine peace and comfort starting to seep into my mind, body, and soul. While my heart aches and a tear drop flows freely, I am assured that my child is resting safely in the arms of Jesus. Maybe he can even see the scars in our Savior's hands and feet and know that his acceptance of the salvation offered him through Jesus Christ was the best decision he ever made. This is from the view of a mother.

In preceding chapters, I reference the "Widow of Nain," the mother whose only son died and was a widow. I said she would be referenced again as her story did not end with her walking next to her son's body as it was being carried. The Lord Jesus saw her and had compassion on her and said unto her, "Weep not" (Luke 7:13, KJV).

In Luke 7:14-15 (KJV), "And he came and touched the bier: and they that bare him stood still. And he said, Young man, I say unto thee, Arise. And he that was dead sat up, and began to speak. And he delivered him to his mother."

Jesus touched the coffin that enclosed the body of this young man and said, "Arise." The young man that was dead sat up and spoke. Jesus then presented him to his mother.

What an extraordinary witness in the scripture. This mother saw the authority and power of Jesus as He touched the coffin of her son and told him to "arise." The joy she must have experienced.

Although the Lord did not heal my son and command him to 'arise' physically from his sick bed and present him to me, his mother, there was a calling on November 1st, that only my son could hear. The call was to his spirit and soul to arise. Most probably he would have heard it and seen angels who were appointed to escort him to his destination. I did not experience joy on that day but I do so feel and experience it now.

My fellow traveler, Jesus sacrificed His life for us, every human being. "For God so loved the world, that he gave his only begotten Son, that whosoever believeth in him should not perish, but have everlasting life. For God sent not his Son into the world to condemn the world; but that the world through him might be saved" (John 3:16-17, KJV). Jesus left the majestic glory of Heaven, willingly, to fulfill an assignment given by His Father, God. "For I came down from heaven, not to do mine own will, but the will of him that sent me" (John 6:38, KJV). Jesus physically suffered more than our minds can possibly imagine. He died on that cross, sacrificing His life, just to atone for our sins. He became our substitute. He died to save my child, He died to save you, He died to save me, and He died to save mankind. He paid the price for our sins so that we can be forgiven and be placed in the right relationship with God the Father.

A promise was given, a sacrifice was carried out, the salvation was accepted, and in the presence of the Savior the promise is being experienced. Hallelujah! Praise the Lord! My son has arrived at his heavenly destination for all eternity.

That same inheritance is available to all who have faith and believe. We do not want those we love and others to leave this earth without being introduced to Jesus Christ. Even during times of sorrow and brokenness, by way of our testimony we are to witness to the unsaved. I encourage you to reach out to others and spread the gospel, "the Good News," to all that will listen. If you have not accepted Jesus Christ as your personal Savior then it is time for you to decide. Life can end in a blink of an eye and each of us needs to know the address of our destination where we will spend all eternity.

A resurrection has occurred, and it is mine. A rising from the ashes of sorrow and heartbreak to a newness of life. A new season in my life, I am surrendering to the will of God so that His purpose for the rest of my days on this side of Heaven will be accomplished. "Being confident of this very thing, that he which hath begun a good work in you will perform it until the day of Jesus Christ" (Philippians 1:6, KJV).

What is the address of your destination?

Journal Pages

_____

_____

_____

_____

_____

_____

_____

_____

_____

_____

_____

_____

_____

_____

_____

_____

_____

_____

_____

_____

_____

_____

_____

_____

_____

_____

_____

_____

_____

_____

_____

_____

_____

_____

_____

_____

_____

_____

_____

_____

_____

_____

_____

_____

_____

_____

_____

_____

_____

_____

_____

_____

_____

_____

_____

_____

_____

_____

_____

_____

_____

_____

_____

_____

_____

_____

Epiphany: My Testimony, Anointing, and Purpose

I started this book with a declaration and will end it with the same: God is my Father; Jesus is my Savior; and the Holy Spirit is my helper. The Lord is 1st in my life.

Just because we are Christians, we are not immune to events happening in our lives that present hurt, heartache, sickness, loss. I have had my share of loss, as you may have had. If you have not experienced it yet, you will, unless the Lord calls you into eternity first. I wrote earlier in this book that when I visit the cemetery and leave through the exit gate, I feel a sense of dread and sadness, still today. My families' earthly bodies are there, their presence is with the Lord, and I am heading home.

My epiphany is that I have been left behind because the Lord has an assignment for me. I did not appreciate those who said that to me after my son passed. A comment made without insight. Yet, there is truth in that statement, which came to light when the Holy Spirit guided me to write *Crossing the Bridge to Hope and Heaven*.

Each of us process loss differently, but we can be assured that the Lord will carry us through. Circumstances may differ, but God's attributes and character remain the same. The Lord is the same yesterday, today, and forever (Hebrews 13:8). He loves us and is love (1 John 4:8b). He is with us, goes before us, stands beside us, comforts us, and has compassion as we experience the heartaches and hardships of life.

The journey may not be the same each time we experience the death of someone who we love dearly. Case in point, I processed my husband's death differently than my son's. My husband, pastor, preacher, missionary, to sum up his ministry, passed from life to eternal life suddenly one Sunday morning in the pulpit during church service. The Lord called him to Pastor his home church in the last season of his life and it was in that same pulpit where he was licensed and ordained many years before, that the Lord called his name to come home. He was walking "worthy of the vocation wherewith ye are called" (Ephesians 4:1, KJV). After the initial shock to my inner being, I saw the love of God so perfectly. He took him (like Enoch) quickly while he was in God's service in the place where the ministry began. It was my husband's last sermon to the congregation he so loved, and it was a visual sermon.

As you know from reading this book, my son's passing occurred differently. I saw sickness and suffering. However, the love of God abounded on that day, as well. It just took me a longer time to realize it.

I was anointed by the Holy Spirit to write this book, not of myself or for myself. It is for the glory of God. May you reflect and write your experience as you journey through the grief process. Put your complete trust in God, pray without ceasing, hold on to your faith, and lean on the everlasting arms of Jesus Christ. Know that there is life and joy again after loss.

If this book helps even just one person navigate the path of loss, then I know that I have been obedient to the calling for which I have been assigned.

Remember if a person is in Christ, when they close their eyes for the last time, there is assurance, based on the Word, the Bible, that their address is heaven. "Believe on the Lord Jesus Christ, and thou shalt be saved" (Acts 16:31, KJV).

Sure and certain of eternal life in Christ Jesus,

Patricia Ann

Grief Ministries

If you lead a grief ministry in your church or other setting, may I offer you to consider using *Crossing the Bridge to Hope and Heaven* as a tool and resource. Encourage those who have experienced loss to write their own story in the journal pages and use the Word of God to help them navigate through the pain and sorrow to reach hope, healing, and wholeness. If the Church does not have this type of ministry, then I pray that God lays it on the heart of your pastor to consider the birth of one.

May the use of *Crossing the Bridge to Hope and Heaven* help others through the "Mile Markers" of their journey.